CHEAP HOTEL PHILOSOPHY

TEODORA MIȘCOV

Made in London, United Kingdom
2022

Cover art by Bianca Florea.
Published by Kindle Direct Publishing.
ISBN: 9798849079790

www.teodoramiscov.co.uk
Instagram: @Teodora_Miscov
TikTok: @Teodora_Miscov
Email: teodora@teodoramiscov.co.uk

The angels are laughing, but I don't know why
The arrogant, happy, privileged circle
God has his favourites, and it's never I
To his perimeter I'm always — external

I raise my voice and God darts his silent gaze
His dagger of pride, interdiction, and reprimand
Me and the fallen have had to find our own ways
To make up an existence — outside his command

So I live amid my own Gods and Monsters
An actor of my own small mythology
I wonder why they're still singing the gospels
And who can still love their inaccessible melody

This is my philosophy, awake, stuttering, dancing
Outside of the dominion of Heaven or Hell
Morally in danger of always collapsing
Less of a kingdom and more of a dirty hotel

From my unmade bed I can still sometimes hear it
The call of perfection, of God and his angels
Sometimes even I tire of this cheap linen
And of always explaining myself to these strangers

But I like the motorists, they're nice enough
And I get a free drink or two now and then
God promises much more, but I call his bluff
Always ending my evenings with a hearty *'Amen.'*

I see you're trigger-happy
And I get it. I would be, too
Your voice is sounding raspy
One pack a day will do that —
Mine is, too

If you're just like me, you share my vices
I'm too quick to love, I crave connection
Look at my speech, it just comprises
Soft words that avoid aggression

I'd rather starve than swallow this weakness
It hangs metallic on my chest
I thought my silence was forgiveness
But it's really anger unexpressed

It feels like now's the time for retribution
But this war is too bloody, ugly, tense
Although I've not the strength nor inclination
There's no more time for blind pretence

Much too proficient at delusion
I'll learn to clear the air around me
This is a quiet sort of resolution —
I'll say it once, I'll say it loudly.

I wish that I could speak in symbols
And draw a spiral, black, to show you dirty water
But all I've got is broken riddles
In which every other word rhymes with 'father' —

No matter. I'll still write these signs for you;
Sentences, lines, abbreviations
I'll leave you my cheap philosophy as a clue
It may transcend some limitations

This way, I feel that way you may know me,
The me beyond sheen and physicality
Although we're separated by more than one degree
And the treachery of personality.

As a bird that might circle in whichever direction
As a person who may choose to stay or to leave;

As much a part of this world as is the wind,
Flying high in the sky like an ace in a sleeve;

As a swallow sighted in the absence of summer
As an agent of free will and a killer of dreams

As a creator who destroys as well as redeems
As a balanced individual who resides inside extremes

Me, as a mere human clothed in second-hand jeans
Me, as a caricature of the self with friend figurines

Ripping in the centre,
I stay intact at the seams.

Some of the games we play are deadly
Still, you bare your neck as I expose my chest
What's love for one is love for many
No one knows me, but you may know me best

What's tonight if it's not blessed?
What are our lives if not bewildered chance
Charred by the chaotic fumes of lewd affairs
And an acidic dash of nonchalance?

I say, a snake charmer is a charmer nonetheless
And if I must be your snake, let me be venomous and vile
If you want to know my name, then you must guess
You know to be straightforward's not my style.

Wish I could play in the neighbourhood park
Flower crowns, velvet dresses, soft curls
White days and knock-off Eastern Fanta
Nothing to do but be the quiet one of the girls

I miss my father's steady hands
To hear his voice decide my plans
I miss the earth that held my weight
Now all I do is oscillate

Sometimes I want somebody to tell me what to do
When my hands start shaking, I need to look up to you
But then your hollow words remind me how little anyone knows
And how ill equipped most of us are to handle life's blows.

God dropped the Sun
And it fell on our heads
But still, we never bow them —

We hold them upright
As each pretends
We're not just made of carbon

Maybe this is us
And this is what we must do
Bear that things do not get better

Maybe this is it
And this is the truth:
We must hold the Sun forever.

I come from nowhere, I am no one
Followed the highway West and it led me to a brave new world
Spent five years here, not having that much fun
(Should have left after the third)

When do we draw the line?
When is enough enough and when is it much too much?
I'm not sure I was even looking for a sign
I think this city held me in its clutch

I must have thought I was happy here
And I think I was, but not quite enough
I thought I'd stay and make it big
Now the sheer thought of if makes me laugh

Still, I wouldn't have it any other way
I've grown to love this cruel butterfly effect
Whether I leave, whether I stay
No choice ever proves itself correct.

Have you felt the loss of faith
That makes you cower in the sand —
That makes you turn miracles into equations
So your mind can better understand?

Perhaps it's human, after all
We live, we doubt, we come around
Even Satan had his fall
Maybe he believed by the time he hit the ground

In this epic narrative
Fought by angels who rebel
God's word is no longer imperative
Worth less than a fake Chanel

Well, to hell with it —
I've got no answers, how about you?
I've lost my skill for subterfuge
And I've no man to look up to.

You're the rose that grows
Independent of the shrub
When you smile like that, it shows
You don't feel part of the club —

You've learnt the games
And walked the walk
But I know you're still in doubt;
I can hear it when you talk

If you feel so out of place
Why do you still hang around,
Thumping your swollen heart on locked up gates
Watching it bleed out on the ground?

Only my dreaming keeps me awake
Eyes deceive the most when open
I'd talk to you, but you won't relate
My reality becomes less real when spoken

This language I doubt that you could comprehend
You'd conjugate with hundreds of dilutions
So I'll keep its syntax safe inside my head —
I never cared too much for crude intrusions.

My kisses are obscured by the moon
And the dark feels the hardest to lose
While I sit around waiting for June,
I love. Keep a touch of my blues.

The night is young, let's hear a bit of rock
And pour some sugar on this waste of space
You always light cigarette after cigarette
Does it make you feel less out of place?

The best thing there is to do
Is play some music and really fucking hear it
The future's much too far and out of view
It feels so incoherent

Did you hear that the horizon is curved
So that we can't see too far down the road?
What a crazy, stunning world
What a puzzle to decode.

I want you to write your summer
In kisses softly traced upon my waist
I wonder how hot it's going to feel,
How much ink you'll deliciously waste

I can already feel the curvature
Of your lines up and down my thighs
Summer's beautiful, but cunning —
Always delivers less than it implies.

Life feels so stupid sometimes
Pages of philosophy hold no consequence
I'm told to watch out for the signs
But to me, it looks like providence

Most of the time, it looks like a whole lot of nothing
Most of the time, I laugh to myself
Some days, I have the power to be trusting
And wait to know what until now has been withheld

But Sisyphus, goddamn, he got one thing right
And Camus figured out he had to be smiling
I myself think he would've had to rhyme and sing
To keep his heart, not arms, from stopping.

I don't like these bruises on my knees
I've turned all purple, red, and blue
I crawled some time to get here
I know it means nothing to you

What's been done is done — whatever
I lived the way I lived
Somehow, I pulled myself together
And still look like some sweet kid.

I used to smoke my straights
Down to the filter
And play Nirvana, Floyd, the Doors
When I was only seventeen
But my slate was anything but clean
I used to hide away in my room for days
Watching films of the life
I couldn't believe I could live
Absorbing emotions through a screen
Taking refuge in art like a true sanctuary
Of what my own life could've been,
If only [   ]

I used to play old vinyls and light up musk incense
Balancing on the edge of my bed
As if off of a cliff
My light blue bedroom didn't seem like much of a battleground
But it was
A full-blown war fought
With despondency and limitation
By a tired, young, directionless bitch
Who had to learn what it's like
To win her life back

Inch

By

Inch.

I smile to the ripeness of peaches
Their juices imbue and persist
Eden is filled with such dirty creatures
And I belong right here in their midst

Why did God despise the snake
When all it did was tempt with truth?
It must be that being honest is a mistake
That knowing reality is somehow too crude

But my questions are both sacred and profane
And terrible, all at once —
I let my cup runneth over with verse arcane
Built in the language of impulse.

Look at you, a babe in the woods
Or so they'd like to imagine —
At first glance, wide eyes and smiles
Hide all the signs of abandon

They may ask how you got here,
But they don't want an answer
All the chinks in your armour
Made them almost want to discover

And yet their words live on the surface
They're afraid to see too deeply
They sense the essence of you
Won't be given away cheaply

They've not the time nor inclination
To see, to love, and understand
So they'll write you off as an aberration
In an equation they'd rather forget

But do you want their prying eyes?
Why would you crave their attention
When all they do is categorise
With a brutal lack of comprehension?

Sweet babe of the woods,
Their vision is blurred, distorted, obscene -—
I pray they never understand you
May you die with your name clean.

A feeling is a feeling is a feeling
And a feeling by any other name
Would still feel as sweet -

It's not about the label,
Life's about the thing

Don't study notes and octaves
And then forget to sing

Remember, and don't be fooled:
Life's only ever about the thing.

It's cold in my room
Sunflowers shiver in the window
I curl up under the covers
And then hug my velvet pillow

So many days I've spent
Stuck in this frozen contemplation
Of what I've done and where I went,
The embarrassment and the elation

I think until my mind refuses
And there are no more facets to analyse
I subject my mind to these abuses
Think of the past, of life, and agonise

And I hear the world outside continue
Lovers of life who live without obsessive introspection
I wonder how it is they get through
All this mindless fodder without asking a single fucking question

I'd rather spend days like this in bed
Thinking about the life of some dead Russian
It at least feels good to not pretend
That it makes sense when it just doesn't.

There's no ocean without passion
Just an endless wave of no distinction —

I like it when your eyes get darker
And your smiling face betrays their contradiction

I even like it when you turn your back on me
You and I know to be in love we must be alone

Reality tends to cut into ideals
Until it hits the fucking bone.

Take me on a ride, I'm on your side
Let's make this into our belle époque
I'm strung up on the safety you provide
So I please you and I don't provoke

I love too easily, like high summertime
'Much too vanilla,' you said — I don't polarise
That's because I've spent too many years with bad valentines
In dubious liaisons and shady car rides

…I say that, but in truth, it wasn't even that bad
When I look back it's almost always with a laugh
The first part of my life got a bit out of hand
But I made it out fine, and now you can't call my bluff.

My visions of Beauty turn into monsters
Something's rotten behind every façade
I've learnt to dance in such distorted postures, but
I'm much too human to create like a God

Artistry and arrogance — and hope beyond all
That these pink pulsating hands have some sort of power
But on days, weeks like these, I feel so very small
And it takes everything I've got not to let myself cower.

If you can hold it in your mind,
Does that make you less afraid?

To define is for the fearful
Meaning is only man-made

You can't imprison life in symbols
Passion doesn't run in Centigrade

There's no formula you can scribble
To win a game that must be played.

Your eyes sense these words
Your mind perceives their meaning
You're the cypher and the code
Look how artfully you're dreaming.

I sleep my way inside a heroin dreamworld of emotion
In which recollections are only allowed on the back of my eyes
I'm like you, I only remember the memories I wish I'd erased
They're the same twelve, but always take me by surprise

What's most frightening about memory
Is that it can feel more real than the present
It's less than a future, but more than a dream
It somehow speaks about what we're destined
Ten thousand variations on the same fucking theme

It's incredibly boring, yet relevant to the extreme
I'm compelled to pay attention, my eyes won't look away
If this is my subconscious, my subconscious is mean
Just another hunter making fun of its prey.

Another Sunday afternoon washes over me
With burnt vanilla, unread Dostoyevski, and fresh cut flowers
I don't know what to do with myself, or where to be
So I watch the candle burn like my hours

Those same children outside laugh and play,
I'm happy for them and their wholesome youth
I know that when the years start passing and passing
The road ahead won't seem nearly as smooth

I feel so lost, I won't even go outside
I may not be able to find my way back home
Suddenly, I feel so afraid
Too much of life is an unknown unknown

The world seems meaner, and death seems so real
I thought this feeling was something I'd outgrow
Maybe these are the wounds that I'll never heal
It's been a while since I've felt so alone.

Summer sings its stupid melody
Do you hear the ice cream truck?
It's hot, I'm heaving breathlessly
Come here, let's get a little drunk

Meet me at our spot, we'll watch the sunset
I like the river, I like the city
Let's get some wine and dance, no stress
Sauvignon makes me feel giddy

Just for today, let me be stupid
I'm my own tyrant, all-or-nothing
I've spent too much time being lucid
I want to feel like I'm a twenty-something.

I wonder which sky will grant me my last freedom
Or if God will hold my hand over the threshold
I wonder if he'll come to me as an eagle
And bring me laughing to a new crossroad

What is life if not a labyrinth of meaning
With a fractal centre of bewilderment?
What can we be led by but our feeling,
Loves so strong they make us arrogant?

I've lived enough great love stories in my lifetime
I've lived enough to write a few stray pages
I'll feel best when I've found what's mine
And I know what's mine will come in stages

In the meantime, I go through my lunar phases
And I kiss you gently to mark each passing season —
Will we stay awake enough throughout life's changes
To bring our vision to completion?

You put your jeans on in the morning,
I like your Wranglers, ripped with hints of blue
You always leave me without warning
I pretend it's fine and so do you

I feel what I feel and there's no stopping
I've a bleeding heart and it bleeds through my shirt
My love was made for Miller's tropic
Reality's seen it drop dead in the dirt

I get out of bed as you pour the coffee
Another day alone, even though I'm with you
I look outside and the air is so foggy
As you and sun rays come in and out of the view.

If I were a priest
I'd baptise in leather tights
Maybe fast during the day,
But drink heavily at night

I'd preach the holy scripture
Of Jim Morrison and ride
From the West back to the East
Smoking purely out of spite

If I'd become a priest —
Well fuck it, I still might —
I'd have a drink with Jesus Christ
And try to get him in a fight

I'd teach him how to shot tequila
Play classics all throughout the night
He might make me a believer
If he could dance, he could be right

In return, he'll show me a God who does more than punish
And repeat his ten hollow commandments,
He'll describe a God I can connect with
Over passion, sex, and imperfections

Maybe he'll show me the Jesus who enjoys life
Perhaps show me some sweet humanity,
Give me truth, but also freedom
And a God who is like me.

There's no softening the coming tide
It comes, it sees, and it destroys
I know you thought the sand had dried, but —
You must meet the unforgiving wave with poise
Chaos brings its spine sensation
When it slurs its snake-like voice
Yet we play the game of transformation
And hope to die as if it's out of choice.

I dream of not being deceptive
But my heart's forgotten how
Can't dispel this code I've built from nothing
I can't break my own law

I started being cryptic
And got trapped within a crypt
I've nothing left but this caked face
And acting out my script.

Human, interrupted —
Clear, yet imprecise
Where do we draw the line
Between what we know
And improvise?
All the rules
And all the games that we devise
Are just cover-ups
We don't want to agonise
Over life and what it means
To be human, to be us

God knows that it takes strength
To look ourselves right in the eyes.

I began where I always do
With a blank page and eager fingers
Compulsively reaching for a pen and for you
Both have gotten me through one or two lonely winters

December in the East is no fucking joke
And I know you're always looking to escape
I'm always looking for art, for domes, for baroque
I need a place that will help me create

This isn't it, that much we know for certain
If what we've got is nothing, then we've got nothing to lose
Very soon God's going to throw down the gauntlet
And really give me a reason to be singing the blues.

Life's days find me loafing in the grass
Admiring Whitman's leaves and God's caress
Things have come and things have passed
I've got your love, I feel that I've been blessed

When the mountains crack open, I will not shudder
Likewise when the heavens fall
In your face I see the blue of summer skies
In my love I hear God's wisdom call

I live within this larger world
With its songs and rites that I hardly understand
I know little of anything but
I understand everything when you hold my hand

We're blessed with youth, we've still got time
To do what we feel we must
So I waste some of it on days like this
And feel you feel me in the grass.

This thing between us —
Well, it's a different kind of war
Fought in dim alleyways at night
When no one's there to keep the score

I graze and taste your gunpowder
I smell aggression on your neck
In the shadow of your willpower
Only love's left to protect.

Still good to be alive
Grateful to have somewhere to drive
Sometimes, even that's not needed —

I'm easy, and you don't need much to go
A black T-shirt and some oud cologne
I know you're not conceited.

The back of your portrait
Screams out what your face conceals

It never escapes your mouth,
But your eyes leak your ideals

Even you may not notice
What you're saying, really, when you speak

The subconscious has this way of playing
Its meanings always stream oblique.

I drown within the sound of silence
Echoes stream like unforgiving waves
The world is cold, but without malice
It destroys and also saves

I wonder what's my place within it
It seems that time made us all its slaves
It breaks our bones and cracks our spirit
Drains the youth coursing through our veins

I think I'll see it when I believe it
But life hides as much as it displays
Why must meaning be a secret?
Why is life an endless maze?

I try to look somewhat human
But in your face, I see I'm failing
If this is the set, then I am Truman
Except I wouldn't mind all the pretending —

If this is the film, then who's directing?
I'm thinking this is more of a Lynchean affair
I'm doing too much sad reflecting
I'm 24 and stupid, down, threadbare

I'm an actor and a poor one at that
My movements are forced and so is my pace
Every line I deliver sounds so flat
My smile cracks the make-up on my face

There's a method to this mess
In the dusty attic of my stupid moods
When to turn right, when to turn left
I've lost it for many, many moons.

Heaven help us
And rise us up to higher highs
Keep us and preserve the truth
When the inner fire dies

Guide us with divine musicality
When nothing else is absolute
Other than God's divine comedy
That stings so cruel it leaves us mute.

I've found my friends inside the cinema
They speak only when the lights are off
Sometimes in lines that sound cliché
Or even flat — I don't mind it, though

All I can see is what they choose to show
I'm at the hand of the projectionist
What's beyond the frame is not for me to know
I guess I'll leave it to the specialists

They tell me stories, and I listen in silence
We've got an arrangement of sorts
Encased in film, they look so timeless
And turn their own transience into photons

Tornatore, Guadagnino, Sorrentino
They keep me up all night and we philosophise
Ogni sera partiamo dal inizio
Inside our bright cinema paradise.

Wrap me tight inside your classical form
Bicep and bravery, curvature and courage
This is our stage, and we must perform
Under these circumstances we must somehow flourish

If life demands it, then we must adapt
With nothing but our values to stand firmly upon
Take this split personality and unite it with tact
Until we finally hear the song of the swan.

Feel like I'm falling into the city
Please hold me tight around the waist
You're so protective when you're with me
I feel so safe close to your chest

This city churns, it never stops
Life feels like speeding on a Harley
I love you baby, love you lots
When I've got you, I've got an army.

We live our lives in little stories
And you, you've got me in our little nook
Burrowed inside our beautiful narrative
In arms so safe they feel like wood.

Babe, you got my sundress so damn wet
I'm drenched in orange juice and mango pulp
The sweetness spreads around my chest —
Can you taste it in your mouth?

You're all warmth and light and lemon zest
When our days go like this, they're the best
My orchard's ripe, your flavour blessed
I knew I had to come out West

Here the summers burst with glory,
Perfumed with sweet fecundity —
I've found the soil that can enrich me
Even through your ferocity.

On days like this the horizon's darker
I live through echoes of Springsteen
With you, I'll go further
It's a sure bet — that's what I mean

I wish that I could be more sweet
Men like you just want to roam
But I'm not the kind who will compete
My heart's cashmere, snags on your chrome

If you want to stay, then stay
And if you want to leave, take care
I'd rather you be on your way
Than rip in me what I can't repair.

We dream up hopeful plans
While God watches and laughs
Baby, I say fuck it,
Might as well just take that chance

We're children of blind circumstance
Who learn to adjust
Just as the tide turns

Maybe I'll learn to watch and laugh too
While the whole damned thing burns.

When hands are wrinkled
The film all wrapped up
The meaning unriddled,
The credits rolled out,

What has been framed
In the director's vision,
Which actors unnamed
And left to derision?

What did you show,
What did you not,
And where did you keep
The you that didn't make the cut?

I stutter on my every other word
Except for those that are taboo
I don't think we got it right just yet
But I'll take a chance — fuck it — will you?

Take your time. I'll dream up a new dictionary
To be funny, I'll get our names to rhyme
And what if I replace 'crazy' with 'visionary'
Would that make me worth your time?

A cigarette smoked
Half-
        -way
And forgotten
On the edge
Of a full ashtray;
Afternoons
Turning on a bed
Unmade
Face against the covers
Muscles sleeping still;
Books
And bookmarks
Observing, protesting
Demanding a reader
Sentences unfinished
Dozing off after a comma,
Comatose,
Plenty of those,
The dull remembrance
Of days to come
Of things not done
Of poems begun
And never finished —

It feels nothing like it felt before
It changed halfway through a sentence
I open my mouth, but the full-stop isn't guaranteed
We're so damned mutable and that's our essence

Between us and others there is no difference
There's no real ideal and that's the consensus
I thought that we were somehow precious
I guess at least in disappointment, life's always endless

I'm trying to stay sane, but this world
Is nothing like what I thought it was
I feel like I've been roughed up and hurled
In the abyss by the caprice of the Gods.

I looked for you
And found your passion
It feels as good as deadly sin

I grew new roses
From my thorns,
But they smell like everywhere I've been.

One thing I've learnt is that
You should always be ready to leave
And never need more
Than half a tank of gas
And if you're lucky
Two cigarettes —
One for the beginning of your journey
And one for when you realise
You haven't gotten
Nearly
As far as you thought.

No such thing as standing still
The tension always creeps towards the end

Kiss me, it won't make a difference
Either way, we're both condemned

So why don't you be the one to take the arrow?
Lean back deeply, do not stall

Make it real and raw and unapologetic
Not a quiet curtain call.

Nostalgia.
A new spring of wide-eyed hope
Doesn't it feel like we've done this before?
The seasons repeat, and deep in my core
I promise myself change — but then wonder what for.

The prospect of deception
Has never felt so sweet
To walk and not feel faint
To stand on strong, firm feet

To know that his kingdom is mine
And that he makes all my paths straight
To sleep within his trust,
To rest in perfect faith

To celebrate Life
Through artefacts of Love
To heal the fear of losing it
Through fate, or chance, or both

To not be fooled, but live the myth
To find the fountain and then — sip.

Fuck the poets,
I'd trust the scientists on this —
Every high predicts a low
And each descent an afterglow

You know that bitter taste
After a last kiss?
The poets never
Fucking said this:

Learn to master the art
Of intelligent bliss
Only be as happy
As reality permits.

Fake love reeks of sulphur
I like it better when it dies
Cut-throat bluntness gives me comfort
Only the weak find rest in lies

You feel differently, but you say nothing
Why do you pretend to be the same?
That fire inside is always shifting
Its laughter makes you say its name

You're not you anymore and there's no use pretending
We're both transformed, never meet as before
Feelings are either growing or they're fading
Only stay the same in the soul of the whore

And even then, they don't — not really
For all the whore does is numb and forget
When you're with me, I beg you to feel freely
Tell me the truth, even the one you regret.

Red lipstick, red wine nights
My evenings run away from me
Crystal glasses, Crystal on ice
The going's is tough, but so are we

I expect to reach the heights
But when I'm low, Goddamn — I'm low
On good days, I loathe any advice
On bad days, can you take control?

If cherries turn bitter,
What will happen to us?
The sweeter the fruit,
The sooner the rot

I'll smear lime all on my thighs,
Maybe rub my breasts with lemon zest
So you can bite me like the ripest fruit
And keep me sweet against your chest.

I used to love this black tar heartbreak city
More than fresh air, I liked it gritty
I used to pray to the subway for a swift escape
Looked upon commuters like a success parade
With skies of office ceilings, with cigarettes for kisses
Thursday night drinks for lack of a better Christmas
Sticky Soho pavements promised me something great
Clicking under my heels the song of a better fate
And the friends, the lifestyle, the jazz nights out in town
Clinking glasses to drown out sadness, to escape the Hound
Which I was so sure I'd outrun, if only my paycheck were bigger
But success is not success if there's always a higher bidder
And I learned that, if nothing else — I learned a thing or two
When I was waiting for the Central line home to take me
somewhere new
It always took me to the same white walls, or nowhere at all
But it all looks somewhat brighter if you shot some alcohol
And doesn't it all look so much better?
We've made it further, haven't we?
From the East all the way out West — I guess it could've been
much worse
I was on a one-way fast track journey to divorce
Another cog in the dreamless workforce
I was becoming jaded, oversexed, perverse,
I looked much better than I was
Although I still live in this black tar heartbreak city
Ruthlessly ridding me of any trace of fairytale world Disney
I say I'll turn out better, I say I'll get out quickly
I say I'll do my best, but now my best is cutting in me.

Perfection lives inside grimy jazz bars
And stands up on shaky, sticky tables
It shouts and tunes you into raw emotion,
Its highs, its lows, and fluctuations

Perfection lives in basement bars
It stays alive through generations
Propagated through musicians' lonely hours
And eavesdropping on their conversations

Perfection lives on whiskey and peanuts
You can see it at the end of the night, passed out
It lives the way it lives and that's its genius
It is what it is and it knows what it's about.

When I finally find out where I'm from
I'll buy myself a round
Pray to my own version of the Bible
Don't care if I made anyone proud

I want to hear nothing but my own original language
Awaken the knowledge within
Then toast in the Garden of Treason
To my own original sin.

Some days leave me uninspired
And I fall back to the same damn themes
Of God and angels, of melancholy,
Of childhood and the death of dreams

I bore myself sometimes, you know
When I see me write these things
And I erase line after line
Hoping it'll force fresh water springs

Tonight I'll go down to the river
Hold my little paper cup and wait for torrents
I won't get bored, I have some liquor
Maybe I'll think something of importance —

Blood's thicker than water
But not thicker than your cheap whiskey and smoke
I heard you say it, but I don't think it's true —
Is all fair in love and war?

I look at it as a baptism of fire
To run, an impulse we should never ignore
But when it mattered most, I was as still as Pygmalion's statue
All marble and stone except for my core.

If the fruit looks sweet, then bite it
You never know, you just might like it

When you hear the snakes rattling
That is how you know you're close

Once more to feel that honey dripping
From your open lips down to your toes

Oh, to soak that heat that leaves you shivering
When the height of pleasure goes.

I'm the Madonna and the whore
With appetite carnivorous

My mouth half opened, love galore
Your little girl's turned frivolous.

You say you want to fight,
I sing 'Born to be Wild'

The words have made it outside
I write your white line and watch them ignite

It hurts but I like it, please pour me more wine
Let's laugh at the losers in us

If they're not yet dead,
At least they're left far behind

I say we're born for this,
And this is our ride

Your love makes me bleed from my nose —
Violent out of spite.

Meet me at the L'Immortelle
I'll be there with a Negroni in hand
You've taken plenty of time
To make up your mind, see where you stand

As for me, I'm here — as sure as ever
In my ocean there's no changing tide
I think even when we're worse, we're better
The safest place is always by your side

Our love mimics nature,
Punishing and generous
I've finally lost my young arrogance
To think any of this is effortless

It's not, my love, but that's adventure
It demands the hero in us to fight
I'll be here no matter the weather
I can read our future even in the absence of light.

Our lives, the great opus of a violent master
Fate hit us hard, it will hit again
And yet we've learnt to endure our safe disaster
Then play a score of Beethoven.

Today may be the day
The valkyries ride their waves closer
We always knew:

One day, Sisyphus must drop his boulder.

At some point, the weight of the world will tip over.

Atlas will shrug, and the globe will slip off his shoulder.

The call to adventure is the same as the call to departure
And departure itself is a call to great danger —
When it gets this close it's the time to play some old Wagner
And welcome the valkyrie as though she were an archangel.

Men like you command with grunts,
Please, allow me to obey
I love how your voice sounds —
It makes me feel afraid

I see in you everything
And everything is in your chest
You've left me your fingerprints
Smeared dirt across my breast

All this is yours to claim
There is no use in feigning virginity
I'm drawn like a moth to a flame
By your raw masculinity.

When you speak to me
It sounds like it's in Ampère
You make it hot
Make it electric
I can taste it in the air.

I'm the one who's always leaving
But now I've got an arm around my neck
I keep looking for some kind of safety —
Must our paths diverge after they intersect?

These affairs come and go, always leaving me sleeping
In a night that's as long as I'm used to neglect
If life's like a train then we're all always leaving
Exploring new worlds with an old dialect.

If I wonder, I want you to wonder with me
Let's explore this strange existence
Is it just inertia, time, and space?
Is this the path of least resistance?

This I know, life is not for cowards
We're worth everything, but not in any form
Can we make it that when we gaze backwards
We see our faith in us restored?

I'll bring my love to Heaven's gate
In collected lines of poetry
I'm tired of being told to wait
I'll wear my finest jewellery
Maybe I will find you there
Joking with Michael and John
I hope you'll be singing your own artistry
We can celebrate with a Chandon
Or maybe with a sweet chanson —
Promise to break the rules we've grown to hate
Your soul, my soul, whatever they may be
Will learn to not ingratiate
And swim calmly in the sea.

Don't you trust those dragging feet
You'll get home safely tonight
I know that their words feel heavy
And I know what's on your mind

The perfect storm that's in your head
It also keeps me up at night
I know that when the past comes rushing through
Even Matisse looks black and white

Trust that laughter will sound true
And things will start to feel more light
Someday, I'll believe it too
Until then — another night.

I hear you walking outside my door
And I love you, stranger, so there we are
I like how you remind me I'm not alone
You're my bestest friend, by far

I wish that you'd say more, though
Your steps are comforting, but oh so light
There's never any knocking on my door
You must be busy, I know — alright

It's my fault, really, I came here alone
Left my absence at home to grow absence around me
But my hand is always reaching for another to hold
I've been here for much longer than I thought I would be.

I find God cuddled inside my bed
On cold September mornings like this one
I'd like to let my fears fall in his hand
But I know better than to ask

So I'm quiet, mostly, I don't speak
When I talk to him, my words are convoluted
I want him to think I'm unique
But the truth of me comes out compulsive

I'm of the world, and the world is of me
I belong and yet I don't
I imprison myself even though I could be free
I could leave but I just won't

Me, I am who I am and who he made me
A mistress with pretensions of the favourite child
Curled up in my bed on early mornings
Writing lines for him inside of my mind

Even the bitterness can taste sweet
Do you choose to see a love bite or a sore?
If this is it, I might as well love it
I've tired out swimming against the tide before.

However painful, we must live the way we must
Be it out of passion, or out of coercion
What needs to be said cannot be hushed
Truth leaves room for no other option

So spare me your complexes,
A waste of time, a waste of life
If you'd let go of pretences
You'd find yourself on the edge of a knife

With nothing to hold on to but fear
Nothing to keep warm but anger
Even your love reeks insincere
Even your love declarations are slander

Time has passed, but not made you a man
You've grown older, but not become who you should've
Nestled in a man-child dream world, Peter Pan,
Doubting in old age what you once were so sure of

I see you try to cover emptiness with lust
A vacuum of values needs to be fed volumes of pleasure
Whiskey and sex won't make you robust
Not living life right was your fatal error.

To be young is to be fallible
Twenty-somethings, age of folly
As easy to be over-emotional
As it is to drink my morning coffee

Mistakes and fuck-ups galore
Force me to admit I'm human
But everything I've done before
I had to do to grow into a woman

I know that my heart is pure
And I know my intentions
I know what God thinks of me
So I'm not afraid of misconceptions

You may make your own conclusions
And I'll accept whatever they will be
It's a messy thing to go through evolutions
When I'm the queen of mutability

With time, I'll be more stable
But it's this energy that defines me
Sometimes destructive, sometimes playful
And it doesn't act out shyly

I've said what I said
But the fuck-up helped me grow
Yesterday me is dead
Now that I know what I know

To be young is to be foolish
Twenty-somethings, age of idiocy
But you know how warm my heart is
And that when I fuck up, I do so lovingly.

It's beautiful to just lie like this
Our Sunday mornings, domestic bliss
Talking about who we've been and what we've done
Walls we've torn down one by one
Cigarette after cigarette, smile after smile
What I've had to do to call you mine
You know I'm dreaming up a life for us
Tending to our garden of roses and thorns
We've got so much left to discuss
About this crazy world and the way that it runs
But first, one more kiss, and say you love me
With your deep voice, like you do
It sounds so permanent, like it's proclaimed
Like it's never been more true
Like all we've lost has been regained
Because now you know I love you too.

I grew up with Beethoven
He taught me that the world was beautiful and broken
And when its chaos finally gaped open
It found me shaken, but not frozen

I've learnt about pain through others
And through their art I felt my heavy heart
I learnt of suffering through the colours
Of Goya, Bruegel, Basquiat

Then as a bird pondering upon existence
From a point above, removed —
Now I've lost the luxury of distance
I'm on the ground, I'm burnt, I'm bruised

As a child I heard Für Elise
And I loved its simple melody
Now I feel her cruel caprice
Because I sense it within me.

Even Hell can be enjoyable
If you speak a little Latin.

We walk through streets of representation
From sadness and anger to awe and elation

We see in them what we sense within us
And pretend there's something left to discuss

In fact, we've made our minds up long ago
To see what we see and to know what we know

If we're honest, it'll take some miracle to change
All the ideas we've fought so hard to arrange.

The Nile flows towards the South
And moonlight is the Sun, veiled
Within nature there is no doubt
Physics earth never betrayed

And so the dust within my bones
Obeys the same forces and laws
Be it hearts or be it stones
Be it hands or be it paws

I am the stuff your perception's made of
Its dirt and grime nonetheless
But within this mire, there is love
There is hope, there is success

And when I die, as sure as North is North
And as miraculously sunlight glitters
My trace will be of no import
Lost in torrents of winners, sinners

Like a faint wind on summer evenings
What has been will sure be lost
Still, I can't help but make up these meanings
And philosophise like Robert Frost

So I'll leave you my Energy
A heart filled with love for endless folly
I've grown to praise this entropy
I see the chaos and it's Godly.

My tired eyes are searching for whiteness
In milk glasses, linen shirts, next to your iris

I built a whole personality around this,
I know how to best act when in a crisis

Yet something's missing, possibly my will
To open my eyes when it's easier to sleep

When reality is this bleak, God only knows
Even the wolves consider living like sheep

But never I, never us, it's not in our blood
We lack the cowardice of lounging on the beach

When the tide is coming in so strong,
God feels close; maybe even within reach.

It's been more
Than one hot summer
On the playground

I know the smart way
To fall and scrape my knee

I've made up my mind to go,
Anywhere but homebound

Are you ready?
Come with me –

I do not lament the twists of fate
The narrative of soul, the story of the mind
The only language that we can translate
Is the horror that leaves us all maligned
Suffering corrodes, but it also strengthens
What if I declare I love my pain?
I wish for death to find me without repentance
With fists tight, yet free of strain.

I never knew how to talk to you. Not really.
We were so young and so mean and silly
We turned into women as we grew up together
In a choir of voices wondering whose was better

There's such cruelty in youth, in young womanhood
Learning to walk in heels, learning how to look good
All while surviving all of the damage we could
On our way to escape a fragmented and bitter childhood

No doubt, you were in a sense just like me
And I loved you as you were, because I could see
There was hurt in your heart and it arose as anger
You were just a young woman in need of an anchor

Today I saw you happy and it made me so grateful
And I love you even now, although we don't talk
I hope you're not feeling resentful
And still think of me sometimes when you hear Bach.

We live inside divine architecture
That our hearts explore, that minds corrupt
Life can't be lived inside rhymes and structure
But I love the space it allows us to construct

There is great beauty, there is true valour
It's lived outside these black fallen columns
It's our human perception that gives it true colour
It holds the true scent of our wins and our sorrows.

Every day I look at the world
And through this narrow window I see
How little of life can be observed
How little I understand what it means to be free

What I thought of as liberation
Now looks like an open prison to me
Society keeps messing up my perception —
It tricks me to keep saying 'yes' and agree

Tell me, if the whole world is mad,
Then what does it mean to be called insane?
I've never seen a sheep take a stand
But they don't thrive, they just die off and wane

They die dumb and confused like Ivan Ilyich,
Having lived life as others said they should
I'd rather die alone and poor in a ditch
Knowing I've lived as free as I could.

I write myself inside full stops. and commas,
And sometimes wide parenthesis[
Other times, at the bottom of long letters
As a timid P.P.S.
(Which I hope and think no-one will read -
But the chance is slim, I guess
Especially with readers like you
Whom I don't even know how to address)
At my worst I'm just a lorem ipsum
At my best, an asterix*
Better yet, a formal dictum
Or hidden away inside an obscure page six
Today I do not want to be read
Today I want to be looked over
So if you would be as kind to not proceed —

I like it when my dress it too short
And the wind makes it ride up
I like it when the air is fucking hot
And your lips taste like the cheap drink I got

I can't wait to see you tonight
The week had me feeling kind of lonely
I painted my nails turquoise, dressed tight
So you can go ahead and phone me.

All this virtue, all this game
A life constructed to keep me tame
I'm thinking of playing the bad guy
I keep forgetting — I'm going to die
I can't be held down by my shame
So much of my picture's inside another person's frame
Why do I feel like I need an alibi?
I should just leave and let chaos intensify.

It's like eating cocaine
Like smelling success
Like speaking pure truth
Or tasting decadence

Like seeing the roses
Behind the disgrace
And sensing the beauty
That even decay can't erase.

I've got no aces up my sleeve
Nor do I have any largesse —
The most you'll find on me
Is some old stale cigarettes

But fuck it, I want to raise the stakes
All I want to hear is 'yes'
I'm feeling reckless and ungrateful
I need it all in sick excess.

One woman, one word
The absurd gets more absurd
I live by my aberrant code
Almost blindly, word for word

Away from my old memories
Waltz towards whatever may be
Like the Russians drink their vodka
Rapidly, decidedly

I made a promise to that God
On my honour, on my word
Here stands the Vision reconfirmed
On spilled blood and bridges burned.

Are we ever more than little women,
Are you not still the little girl I knew?
I see you now and remember how I loved you
Your bright lime swimsuit, strawberry shampoo

That blurred, bright summer — '99
The sun, the stream, the games we'd play
Taking in mouthfuls of bathwater
Running, clumsy in the grass all day

There is something about little women
And the simple beauty that they show
Unrefined and raw, alive
With that youthful, rosy glow

I don't think we changed that much
I think we keep that childlike soul alive
Sleeping lightly underneath the surface
As a little silly glimmer in your eye

I see it now in your grown face
A smile that looks as sweet as candy
It's crazy what a difference it makes
To see you laughing, safe, and happy.

And there was the Old Testament,
Written by whoever was on hand
Scribbled slowly, with much care
With a stick in dried up sand —

The children played out on the shore
While their little feet messed up the writing
He didn't say a thing, and neither did they
Neither cared too much for stopping

Somehow going on seemed more important
And, God, how beautiful they were
Their silly games a celebration
Worth more than the most expensive myrrh

If all the prophets had been there,
They would've done just the same
Put those heavy tablets down
And joined in on the game.

White summertime is made for this
Two lovers, friction, and high risk
Don't tell me when the feeling hits —
Just leave its taste across my lips.

I like rolling around on your living room floor
My top taken off and a handful of blow
Maybe I'm just as demented as a rolling stone, but
Don't kiss me like that if you don't want me to moan

You inhale like a winner, like my personal Capone
I like how you're known but also unknown
And I like smelling like you, oud with a dark undertone
So drench me in your manly eau de cologne.

To be great we must be flammable,
Burning souls only refuge in the fire —
We must flame up to our highest octane
And then burn up even harder.

I can fit a life inside this carry-on bag
Watch and learn, I will not sit and wait
You know I'd rather leave and go broke
Than let myself dissolve inside this empty space

I've thrown away much of what I had
And still kept a pocket empty, just in case
I'll meet no one at arrivals,
Best case scenario, you'll meet me at the gates

The red-eye across time zones and meridians
We'll slash the globe with an aberrant dotted line
Departures, early mornings, unintelligible idioms
Human decisions force the stars to realign.

It moves through me like all else does
It comes, it goes, and it escapes —
This thing that I've been searching for,
It takes far too many shapes

I've learnt I'll never hold on to it
There's no satisfaction, just want and desire
I'm addicted to chasing
And this shape-shifting dream's my supplier

So I let it move through me
I let it come, go, and disappear
I've learnt to love its nimbus formations
And not ask it to be clear.

Money isn't the real currency —
In dunes of sand you can't pay your way out
Stop doing things that cheapen your soul
Stop looking for someone to console
Quit your playing, and quit your crying
Build your integrity and build your dignity
Hell creeps in when you find yourself lying
About the nature of life and your capability.

There's tyranny in the compass
And its distorted, perfect arch;
How arrogant to think that what surrounds us
Can be measured with a watch

The scientist in his ordered room
Praying to the Gods of Reason
Dreaming of the right equation
That'll bring his nightmare to completion —

I love him as I love the artist
And I know the void he's feeling
To heal it we will need a wider canvas
And imperfect, dirty pigment.

Heaven is built on human architecture
So dream up your own palette of meaning
The world meets us in a call to great adventure
If we can figure out just what we're feeling —

I think life likes us best when we are singing
Or happy, grateful, loving, true
I've had my share of doom and gloom
I've had enough of feeling blue.

There is such Great Beauty
In your voice, I hear it often
Dancing barefoot to Debussy
In your dress, white, made of cotton

Put your hair up with inattention
I love your offhand carelessness
The world is chaos, no exemption
You're my nymph of negligence

You've shown me Wilde and played The Doors
I've seen you grow like Daedalus
Through all those summers spent indoors
We could never find no one like us

You've grown beautifully and I'm so glad —
We've been through some real dirt in our youth
I know rain used to make you sad,
But you grew up and you learnt the truth

You know so much now, and I do too
We've seen shooting stars on Grecian islands
Part of me now I owe to you
We've both grown up with proud defiance.

Don't misunderstand my coarseness
As rigidity, as coldness —
I want you to know what real love is
Instead of getting the idea it's just a woman
With a bleeding heart in her hand.

Sometimes I know the answer, but I still ask because I like the deep bass in your voice. It vibrates through your chest and into my skull. I feel it there and I hold it there, echoing you. There's something in your voice that doesn't show in the mirror and it's so uniquely you. You never hear it, but it's there. Sometimes when you laugh, you laugh with your real voice. Sometimes you forget what you think and you sound so free. Did you know how safe you are when you're with me?

Reality selects the good from the evil,
And in that way it is our God —
If we are the divine, our minds are the cathedral
In which the battle of Heaven and Hell is fought

Render to Caesar the things that are Caesar's
And to God the things that are God's
Give the human the pain and the struggle
He's got the strength to hope against all odds

What else is there to do while we're still breathing,
What is the world if not an arena for valour?
What more can we be than victors of meaning,
What more anti-human than to cower?

The journey to Hell is easy
Man takes it with eyes closed
What is it exactly that we see
When the right questions are posed?

Nothing disguises reality
And the awareness of where we fall short
We can stand straight in the Sun
If first we realise we're in the dirt

You must see yourself as you are
Deceitful, vengeful, angry as we all can be
Then there is a chance for redemption
But first, you must allow yourself to see.

What I love is basalt and stone
And marbled, mountainous granite
What I love hasn't grown
It's been here since the dawn of time

What is now has always been
Perhaps not here, maybe in another form
What we are now, we'll always be
No matter how much we transform

I feel encased inside this moment
Like a spider inside resin
Each second, I am frozen
Inside a less than perfect haven

If this is it for now, then that's okay
If this is me, I'll live with that
If I need to be here, then I'll stay
If I need to break, then I'll adapt.

I saw some kids today
Crouched on the corner shop floor
Scouring the reduced section
Calculating what they could pay for

The girl wanted a fashion magazine
The guys wanted to save the money for some fags
I could feel their joy of being eighteen-nineteen
Of holding their future carelessly in their hands

They knew the luxury of their youth —
And all the things they could still ignore
All the fun that they could have
Crouched and dumb in a convenience store

Cash poor, but flaunting their inheritance
Of living these years as they liked
They had an offhand arrogance
Skateboards gliding down the aisle

I'm not old, but they made me feel that way
The past five years have proved me right
I win my battles, and now I need to pay
The price of having made it out alright.

The complexity of man
Coded in letters, numbers, script
Ones and zeroes never triumph
Above the legend and the myth

The courage of man
Defeats that of the odds
And if our arrogance permits
We'll even win against the Gods.

I know summertime is over,
But meet me in the fields just one more time
September always makes me colder
Rethinking what should and can't be mine

This is how I spend my lifetime
Or how I wish it could be spent
With no regard to circumstance
Everything riding on the moment

So can you be here with me,
Present every second, for all the years to come?
Can you live a million moments with me
In this God-like dream of mine?

It takes one thousand poems
To write one word that's true
The snake is treacherous
It moves in and out of view

It's not about the art
It's what it allows you to see —
Have you felt the syntax of you
Through the syntax of me?

We talk endlessly
About what it means to be free
Maybe it's all just expression
Maybe that is the key

Maybe all I'm doing is unwrapping,
Getting out of its way
The truth wants to be said
And I try to obey

It takes one thousand poems
To write one word that's true
But if I ever wrote it
I think you felt it, didn't you?

Meet me down around the riviera
On the fifteenth beach south of my youth
I am drenched in perfume and day-old mascara
And I'm tired as hell, to tell you the truth

I didn't know there was so much to carry
But fuck it, I made it, I'm here, I'm with you
Finally protected, and finally — happy
If everything's fake, then at least this is true.

If words are shards of perception
Then my poems are kaleidoscopes
When you get it, it feels nice
I don't know — it gives me hope

It feels like you might understand
And if you do, others might too
This house was once a no man's land
It feels safe now, so — thank you.

Can you sense the code of language in your skin
Played on your veins like a shrieking violin?

Don't filter your perceptions with hollow ink
No philosopher could ever think the way you think

The subconscious is rich with emotion and love
Nuances of which words could never invoke

Rejoice in a soul that is yours and unique
Honour its beauty — let it not speak.

Printed in Great Britain
by Amazon

41830547R00078